Ethel Le Neve her Life Story with the True Account of their Flight and her Friendship for Dr. Crippen Also Startling Particulars of her Life at Hilldrop Crescent

Anonymous

Ethel Le Neve her Life Story with the True Account of their Flight and her Friendship for Dr. Crippen Also Startling Particulars of her Life at Hilldrop Crescent

Ethel Le Nve - Her Life Story
HAR03439
Monograph
Harvard Law School Library
London: Publishing Office 12, Norris Street, Haymarket, 1910

The Making of Modern Law collection of legal archives constitutes a genuine revolution in historical legal research because it opens up a wealth of rare and previously inaccessible sources in legal, constitutional, administrative, political, cultural, intellectual, and social history. This unique collection consists of three extensive archives that provide insight into more than 300 years of American and British history. These collections include:

Legal Treatises, 1800-1926: over 20,000 legal treatises provide a comprehensive collection in legal history, business and economics, politics and government.

Trials, 1600-1926: nearly 10,000 titles reveal the drama of famous, infamous, and obscure courtroom cases in America and the British Empire across three centuries.

Primary Sources, 1620-1926: includes reports, statutes and regulations in American history, including early state codes, municipal ordinances, constitutional conventions and compilations, and law dictionaries.

These archives provide a unique research tool for tracking the development of our modern legal system and how it has affected our culture, government, business – nearly every aspect of our everyday life. For the first time, these high-quality digital scans of original works are available via print-on-demand, making them readily accessible to libraries, students, independent scholars, and readers of all ages.

The BiblioLife Network

This project was made possible in part by the BiblioLife Network (BLN), a project aimed at addressing some of the huge challenges facing book preservationists around the world. The BLN includes libraries, library networks, archives, subject matter experts, online communities and library service providers. We believe every book ever published should be available as a high-quality print reproduction; printed on-demand anywhere in the world. This insures the ongoing accessibility of the content and helps generate sustainable revenue for the libraries and organizations that work to preserve these important materials.

The following book is in the "public domain" and represents an authentic reproduction of the text as printed by the original publisher. While we have attempted to accurately maintain the integrity of the original work, there are sometimes problems with the original work or the micro-film from which the books were digitized. This can result in minor errors in reproduction. Possible imperfections include missing and blurred pages, poor pictures, markings and other reproduction issues beyond our control. Because this work is culturally important, we have made it available as part of our commitment to protecting, preserving, and promoting the world's literature.

GUIDE TO FOLD-OUTS MAPS and OVERSIZED IMAGES

The book you are reading was digitized from microfilm captured over the past thirty to forty years. Years after the creation of the original microfilm, the book was converted to digital files and made available in an online database.

In an online database, page images do not need to conform to the size restrictions found in a printed book. When converting these images back into a printed bound book, the page sizes are standardized in ways that maintain the detail of the original. For large images, such as fold-out maps, the original page image is split into two or more pages

Guidelines used to determine how to split the page image follows:

• Some images are split vertically; large images require vertical and horizontal splits.
• For horizontal splits, the content is split left to right.
• For vertical splits, the content is split from top to bottom.
• For both vertical and horizontal splits, the image is processed from top left to bottom right.

ETHEL LE NEVE

HER LIFE STORY

With the True Account of Their Flight and Her Friendship for

DR. CRIPPEN

TOLD BY HERSELF

Ethel C. le Neve

ETHEL LE NEVE

HER LIFE STORY

THE HOUSE IN WHICH MISS JE NLNC WAS BORN

ETHEL LE NEVE

HER LIFE STORY

WITH THE TRUE ACCOUNT OF THEIR FLIGHT
AND HER FRIENDSHIP FOR

DR. CRIPPEN

ALSO STARTLING PARTICULARS OF HER LIFE
AT HILLDROP CRESCENT

TOLD BY HERSELF

PUBLISHING OFFICE
12 NORRIS STREET HAYMARKET
LONDON

MISS LE NEVE'S STORY

TWELVE of my countrymen have acquitted me of knowingly assisting Dr Crippen to fly from justice With a clear conscience I can say that their verdict was absolutely just Not until Inspector Dew put his head in at the door of my cabin on the *Montrose* when we were nearing Quebec, and almost startled me out of my wits, had I the remotest idea that anything was seriously wrong

I am told that before my trial many people imagined that I must have possessed some guilty knowledge when I agreed to disguise myself as a boy and leave the country with the doctor If doubt as to my complete innocence should still linger in any mind I hope that the full disclosure of all the dramatic circumstances attending our disappearance which I am about to make will entirely remove it

What I have suffered during the last few months no one can guess It is with some reluctance, indeed, that I can bring myself to tell the story of my recent tragic experience Remembering, however, that I have to begin my struggle in the world once more, I feel that it is due, not only to myself, but to the friends who have stood by me in my trouble, that I should tell the facts as I know them

When I have related my story and I trust, softened the harsh judgment of my critics, I desire only that I may be left in peace. The world-wide attention which the case has aroused has certainly made my future a very difficult problem. But I think I could face it with more composure if I knew that the great public understood my real position

Little more than three months ago I was an obscure typist, earning my living like thousands of other girls in the City. All I wished was happiness, not notoriety. My life had been spent in modest surroundings, and gladly would I have avoided the searching light of publicity

About my early days there is very little to be said. Until I was seven I lived at Diss, in Norfolk my native place. There, I remember, I distinguished myself by my tomboy pranks. Little did I imagine then that I was fitting myself to play the part of a boy in real life. Yet so I was

At that time my chief companion was my uncle, who was on the railway. Nothing delighted him more than to take me to see the trains, and even to this day there are few things which interest me more than an engine. How he used to laugh when he saw me climbing trees, or playing marbles, or shooting with a catapult. For dolls or other girlish toys I had no longing

From Diss we moved to London, and here we settled. When I left school I soon had thoughts of

DR HAWLLA LAL LI CRIPPEN

earning my own living. One of our intimate friends happened to be a shorthand teacher, and it pleased him to give lessons both to my sister and to myself in stenography and typewriting.

When my sister was proficient as a shorthand-typist she obtained an engagement at the Drouet Institute. Here I joined her. Very soon afterwards came Dr Crippen, who was fated to influence my life so strangely.

For some reason the doctor took kindly to us, and almost from the first we were good friends. But really he was very considerate to everybody.

I quickly discovered that Dr Crippen was leading a somewhat isolated life. I did not know whether he was married or not. Certainly he never spoke about his wife. But one day a friend of his called at the office. My sister and I were taking tea with the doctor, which we ourselves had prepared.

"I wish I had someone to make tea for me," said the friend. Whereupon the doctor, with his customary geniality, pressed him to stay, and during the chat over the tea-cups mention was made of the doctor's wife.

When the friend had gone my sister asked the doctor whether he was really married. "It would take the lawyers all their time to find out," was the mysterious reply. That was all he said.

When my sister left to get married I took her place as Dr Crippen's private secretary. With her departure I felt very lonely.

Dr Crippen, too, was very lonely, and our

friendship deepened almost inevitable. He used to come to see me at home. All this and his wife is shrouded in mystery.

But one day she turned up in the flesh for the first time. That was, I suppose, about six years ago, when I was still at the Drouet Institute. Her coming was of a somewhat stormy character. I was leaving the office for lunch when I saw a woman come out of the doctor's room and bang the door behind her. She was obviously very angry about something.

"Who is that?" I said in a whisper to Mr. Long (the assistant who bought my boss's suit of clothes just before the doctor and I disappeared).

"Don't you know?" he said. "That's Mrs. Crippen."

"Oh, is it?" I said, with some surprise.

After that I quickly realised Dr. Crippen's reluctance to speak about his wife. He was obviously not happy at home. In fact, he told me he was not.

Not long afterwards Mrs. Crippen paid another visit to the office, which might have ended tragically. There were more angry words, and just before she left I saw the doctor suddenly fall off his chair. I ran up to him. He was very ill, and I believed that he had taken poison. He told me that he could bear the ill-treatment of his wife no longer. However, I managed to pull him round with the aid of brandy, and we did our best to forget the painful incident. I think it was this, more than anything else, which served to draw us closer together.

But while the doctor was grateful to me for what I did on that occasion, I, on my part, had reason to feel under an obligation to him   When I first went to the Drouet Institute my health was very unsatisfactory   At frequent intervals I suffered severely from catarrh   With infinite patience the doctor treated me for this complaint, and it was entirely to him that I owed my cure

Dr and Mrs Crippen went to live at Hilldrop Crescent just about five years ago   It was at this time, too, that I left home and went to live with my sister in a northern suburb of London   I stayed with her about three years, and then went to lodge with Mrs Jackson at Hampstead   She, I may say, was the only landlady I ever had

About a year after the doctor went to live at Hilldrop Crescent I made my first visit there   It happened that he had gone home, and I had received an important message after his departure, so I decided that I would take it to him

The doctor opened the door to me and asked me to come in   Mrs Crippen, who was in the dining-room below, called up to know who it was

' Miss Le Neve, ' replied the doctor

" Tell her to come down," said Mrs Crippen

She was quite courteous to me, and I, on my part, showed no unfriendliness

As time went on my friendship for Dr Crippen grew, and he became the only person in the world to whom I could go for help or comfort   There was a real love between us

Photo]   [British

BELLE ELMORE.

It was about this time that I learnt of Mr Bruce Miller's affectionate correspondence with Belle Elmore—as Mrs Crippen was known in the theatrical world   By sheer accident I happened to see some of the letters which he had sent her   This, I need hardly say, relieved me somewhat of any misgivings I had with regard to my relations with her husband   He told me often that she was his wife only in name, and that I was everything to him She went her way and he went his

I come now to the events immediately preceding the tragic circumstances of our disappearance together   Here, I think, I must refer to what the judge at my trial described as the " Jackson incident "   My landlady made much of the nervous attack which, she said, I experienced about the end of January   She told the judge that I had come home in a state of great agitation   I was trembling My fingers were twitching   I was unable to dress my hair   She thought, she said, that something terrible must have happened

Now, really, I find great difficulty in recalling the exact incident to which she was alluding   It was no uncommon thing for me to come home from the office in a state of mental distress   The life of a typist-secretary is always a hard one, and I had many responsibilities mentally harassing to a girl of my age and temperament   Many visitors would call during the day, and the doctor, trusting me implicitly, would give me full discretion to deal with them   Therefore, I often arrived home in a highly-strung condition All I know is that the much-discussed incident had no tragic significance

I knew nothing about the dinner given by the doctor and his wife to Mr and Mrs Martinetti at Hilldrop Crescent on January 31 As all the world now knows, Belle Elmore has never been seen alive since

On February 1—the day upon which according to the case for the Crown, Belle Elmore died—Dr Crippen appeared at the usual hour at the office, which was at Albion House New Oxford Street, where he now carried on a dental practice in partnership with Mr Rylance, and where also I still worked in his employ If he had really just come from committing a dreadful crime, if he had administered that poison called hyoscine to his wife, and if he had left her dead body alone at the house, it is certainly remarkable that outwardly at any rate, he was his own calm self Surely we, who knew him so well and every expression of his face, would have noticed at once if he had shown the slightest agitation

On the morning of July 9—many months after the day to which I now refer—the assistant, Mr. Long, was the first to remark that his chief was mentally distressed

"Doctor," he said, 'you are looking very pale What is the matter?"

'Oh, some little scandal!'" was the careless reply

This little scene was of course after the sudden intervention in the case of Scotland Yard, as will be seen later in my story, and it is a point worth noting that, although Mr Long noticed that there was something amiss with the doctor on July 9, he saw absolutely no change in his demeanour on February 1, when, according to the prosecution, there was so much more reason for a haggard appearance I saw the doctor all that day as usual, and worked with him, until he left his office in the evening, when he wished me " Good night " quite cheerfully, and went back to Hilldrop Crescent, leaving me to return to my lodgings in Hampstead

I now come to the morning of February 2, and the vital day in the history of Dr Crippen When I reached the office at nine o'clock in the morning I found on my table a note from the doctor, enclosing two letters One was addressed personally to Miss Melinda May, the secretary of the Music Hall Ladies' Guild (of which Belle Elmore was the treasurer), and the other to her in her official capacity The doctor's note to me ran as follows —

' B E has gone to America Will you kindly favour me by handing the enclosed packet and letters to Miss May as soon as she arrives at her office, with my compliments? Shall be in later when we can arrange for a pleasant little evening "

The packed contained, I believe, the chequebook and other documents which Belle Elmore had as treasurer of the Guild I carried out the doctor's instructions immediately The offices of the Music Hall Ladies' Guild were on the same floor as our own, and I stepped round the passage and handed the packet and letters to Miss May. I recollected that this was the day upon which the weekly meeting of the Guild was held, and I naturally supposed that the letters had some connection with the departure of Belle Elmore. But I really did not think much about the matter at the time, being more interested in the amazing news conveyed to me so briefly by the doctor that Belle Elmore had gone away.

Dr. Crippen was at this time, I supposed, at Craven House, Kingsway where he was interested in another business. I imagined that he had come to Albion House the first thing in the morning, left the note for me, and then gone on to Kingsway. Certainly I did not see him again until four o'clock in the afternoon.

"I have had your note,' I said when he arrived. "Has Belle Elmore really gone away?'

"Yes,' said the doctor. "She has left me."

"Did you see her go?' I asked.

"No. I found her gone when I got home last night.

"Do you think she will come back?'

"No, I don't,' he said, shaking his head.

"Did she take any luggage with her?"

The doctor's answer was: "I don't know what luggage she had, because I did not see her go. I daresay she took what she wanted. She always said that the things I gave her were not good enough, so I suppose she thinks she can get better elsewhere."

I was, of course, immensely excited at this disappearance of Dr Crippen's mysterious wife But, at the same time, it did not altogether surprise me I knew well enough that they had been on bad terms together I knew that she had often threatened to go away and leave him I knew also that she had a secret affection for Mr Bruce Miller, who lived in New York

Although Dr Crippen did not say in so many words that afternoon that his wife had gone to this man, the idea was present in my mind and seemed to explain the situation I could not pretend to commiserate with him He had let me into the secret of his unhappy married life and now that his wife had disappeared it seemed to me best for him, perhaps also best for her He was not in a mood then for a long conversation on the subject, and his reticence I readily understood

A remarkable incident took place after this conversation, and looking back upon it now I see that it was owing to my advice that Dr Crippen did something which afterwards at his trial told against him seriously

When we had discussed the departure of Belle Elmore the doctor thrust his hand into his pocket and drew out a handful of jewels—the jewels which have figured so much in this case

"Look here,' he said, "you had better have those At all events, I wish you would please me by taking one or two These are good, and I should like to know you had some good jewellery They

THE HOUSE IN WHICH THE REMAINS WERE FOUND

will be useful when we are dining out, and you will please me if you will accept them "

I said, "Well, if you really wish it, I will have one or two Pick out which you like You know my tastes "

Thereupon he picked out a couple of solitaire rings, a ring set with four diamonds and a ruby, and a small diamond brooch—"the rising sun" brooch There remained a very large brooch set with beautiful stones in the shape of a tiara, with many rows of diamonds arranged in a crescent, and about half a dozen fine rings

I think I might say here that Dr. Crippen was a real expert in diamonds He often used to show me how to know the relative values of them by holding them up to the light and watching their colour As a result I got to know the different fashions of setting, and could distinguish between those set in London and New York

I then asked what he would do with the remainder, as it would not do to leave them about in the house, and as we had no safe, surely it would be better either to sell them or to pawn them Perhaps the latter course would be best, as he could redeem them whenever he was disposed to do so

"That is a good idea," he said "I will take your advice "

It will be seen, therefore, that Dr. Crippen pawned the jewels purely on my suggestion As far as I know, at that time he was not in financial trouble, tempting him to pawn those jewels immediately, as was suggested in court He often used to say to me, " If this business does not succeed there will be money to fall back upon, as I am sure of a certain amount coming in each quarter from some private property—quite enough to live on

After our conversation, Dr Crippen went straightway and pawned these jewels, and on his return said that they had realised £175

"Shall you be able to get them back ? " I asked, and he said to me, Oh, yes, easily "

Our life continued in its usual way, without any memorable incident for three or four days Then one morning the doctor said he would like to take me to a theatre that night He thought it would cheer us both up I readily agreed, being very fond of the theatre But there was a difficulty

" I am troubled about the animals ' he said "I forgot to feed them this morning Having so much to do, I don't see how I can get up to feed them, and I don't like leaving them all day without food "

I ought to explain that the doctor kept some pets —a number of birds, a couple of cats and a bull terrier, of which he was very fond

" Well,' I said, " give me the key and let me go up I will see after the animals '

" Do you mind ? " he said and then he agreed readily to my proposal and handed over the key It was then, as I have said, at the beginning of February, a few days only after that party with Mr and Mrs Martinetti—a few days only after that hour when Belle Elmore vanished

I ran up to Hilldrop Crescent after lunch, and let myself in by the side door The doctor kept no servant, and I was alone in this empty house There was not a sound inside I went straight to the kitchen, where most of the pets were, and then to the pantry—close to the coal cellar—to fetch the milk While thus engaged one of the cats—a beautiful white Persian—dashed upstairs I at once ran after it, but the faster I ran the faster went the cat I was scared, because there was a very valuable bird in the front bedroom, and the doctor had warned me to keep the cats in the kitchen, in order that they should not soil the upstairs carpets However, after chasing the cat all round the house, I caught it at last, and brought it downstairs, and locked it in the kitchen

I may say that this was my first view of the whole house If a murder had just been committed there were certainly no traces of it I remember now that nowhere was there any spot or stain which arrested my eyes, or anything uncanny to affect my nerves Nothing, except the loneliness of this gloomy and roomy house, and the strange untidiness of some of the apartments

There was evidence, however, of the character of Mrs Crippen here, though she had disappeared Rich gowns lay about the bedrooms, creased and tumbled in disorder Lengths of silk which had never been made into frocks were piled up, and on the pegs was a regular wardrobe, like part of a dressmaker's show-room I learnt afterwards that

Mrs Crippen had a passion for bargain-hunting, and would bring home all kinds of wearing apparel and cheap stuffs, which often she would never trouble to wear Even from my cursory examination that day I was struck by this extraordinary litter

Having left the pets quite happy again, I went out of the house, locked it up, and later rejoined Li Crippen at the office

As far as I remember, I went to live at Hilldrop Crescent about the second week in February During the preceding days I had gone home once or twice, I think, to put things straight From the first I took a dislike to the house It was so big, and, without a servant, I found it almost impossible to keep it as tidy as I should like

In spite of the extravagant way in which Mrs. Crippen dressed and her fondness for personal adornment generally, the house was, I thought, furnished in a higgledy-piggledy way There was scarcely anything which matched The only thing in the house which I liked was the ebony piano All the other things had been picked up at sales by the doctor and his wife, and were of the most miscellaneous description There was a tremendous number of trumpery nicknacks, cheap vases, china dogs, and occasional tables There were lots of pictures—small oil and water-colour paintings by unknown artists—with bows of velvet on them to add to their beauty

However, I made the best of things as I found

them, and I suggested to the doctor that it would be well not to use all the rooms, in order to save trouble So I economised in the household work as much as possible

I used to get through my morning's work as rapidly as I could, in order that I might get to the office, where I still continued my secretarial duties, by about ten o'clock Of course, some days I was a little later, when, for example, I used to do the shopping

I had not been at Hilldrop Crescent very long before I had discovered that Mrs Crippen had left behind not only a considerable wardrobe and the jewels which I have already described, but also a quantity of expensive furs At the same time, I was quite ignorant of the precise belongings of Belle Elmore, and if she had taken a good deal of luggage with her I should not have been any the wiser I had not the least idea what she possessed But that she had left behind so much did not arouse any suspicions in my mind People, I am told, have expressed their astonishment repeatedly that I should not have thought it strange that a woman going away across the sea should have abandoned all her personal property—her clothes, her jewels, her furs—and departed presumably with nothing but the dress she was wearing " Surely,' they have said, "that girl, Ethel Le Neve, must have known that this was wildly impossible '

Good gracious me, I thought it was the most natural thing in the world ! It has always seemed to me that any woman with a spark of pride, any wife abandoning her husband for another man, would scorn to pack up the things which had been bought by one whom she no longer loved, and to carry away what had come to her by marriage So far from being an extraordinary and widly improbable thing, it was surely the most ordinary and common-sense occurrence In this respect I think I have been unfairly criticised by the public Did I not know that she had many times complained to Dr Crippen that the things bought with his hard-earned money did not satisfy her, and that another man could provide her with greater luxuries ? I did not question the fact that she had walked straight out of the house, abandoning her old home life, and relinquishing everything it had contained

After all, as regards the jewels, they had been bought by Dr Crippen as an investment It was impossible for Belle Elmore to have paid for them I have seen her contracts and I know that even when engaged on tour her salary amounted at the most to £3 a week, out of which she had to pay her agent's fee and other expenses How, then, could she have bought jewels worth many hundreds of pounds ? And if the property were not hers why should she take it away ? On this part of the case, at any rate, I think the public have misjudged me, because they have not paused to think

I ought, perhaps, to refer now to the ball at the Criterion on February 26, to which Dr Crippen took me. Neither of us was very anxious to go. The doctor had bought a couple of tickets, and naturally he wanted to use them   He asked me if I would go with him   I said that I was not very keen, as I had not danced for some years, and I had not a suitable dress

Some people have said that I went to the ball in one of Belle Elmore s frocks   Nothing of the kind My dress was made for me at Swan and Edgar s, bought with my own money   All I wore of Belle Elmore's was "the rising sun " brooch, which attracted so much attention   As a matter of fact, Mrs Crippen s big figure and my own small size would have made it absurd for me to put on one of her gowns

After this I noticed that the members of the Music Hall Ladies' Guild were showing marked curiosity in my movements   Often when I went along the street with Dr Crippen I remarked people staring at me in a curious way   "Good gracious ! " I said, "do they think I haven t paid for these clothes I am wearing ? '

In course of time the doctor told me that Mrs Crippen had caught a chill, and had died of pneumonia in America   That would be about the end of March   Trusting him as I did, of course I believed it   He was the man to whom I had looked up for ten years, and he had been the soul of honour to me   I put implicit faith in all he said and did. Naturally I did not know of the letters he was writing to Belle Elmore's friends, which, none the less, corresponded with his statements to me   I **see**

DR. CREAM AND MISS LE NEVE IN THE DOCK AT BOW STREET

.ow they must have served to draw attention
upon us

At Easter Dr Crippen suggested a little holiday,
and, taking merely a valise with us, we went to
Dieppe   There we spent four or five very happy
days   When we returned I had a good deal of
house work to do, though I must say the doctor did
all he could to lighten my labours   He used to come
with me to the coal cellar, scuttle in hand, and
while he was shovelling up the coals I would lean
up against the door holding a lighted candle and
chatting with him   That coal cellar !   I shudder
as I think of it now, though my light laughter
echoed in it then

So time slipped along—both of us extremely
happy and contented, working each of us hard in
different ways   It was our intention to leave London
when our scheme with regard to business should be
completed, and retire to the country, which I love
so well

This would mean the end of business for me
Little did I think then that my—or, rather, our—
plans were not to be realised.

At Whitsuntide the doctor and I went for
another little holiday, this time to Boulogne   I was
very fond of the Continent, and so was he, and, of
course, we enjoyed the change

While we were at Boulogne, Dr Crippen suggested that we should engage a French maid to
accompany us back to Hilldrop Crescent   I have a
fair knowledge of the language, but I am afraid my

pronunciation of it is not all that it should be. It was in order that she might help me in this matter that we engaged our French girl, Valentine and also, of course, to give me some assistance in the housework. She was just seventeen, and, as she had been previously in London and liked it very much, she was delighted to return with us.

I pass now to Friday, July 8, when my trouble began. Until then I had not had an altogether unhappy life. I was young—just twenty-seven—and the cares of life did not weigh too heavily on me, in spite of occasional worries and the daily drudgery, but now all the current of my life was swiftly changed.

On that Friday morning Dr Crippen went to the office as usual at a quarter-past eight, and I worked about the house, making beds and so on, and preparing for the morning's shopping. I was not fully dressed, and had not yet put on my blouse for the day. Suddenly, to my surprise, I heard a rat-tat-tat at the front door. It was then about half-past nine.

"Good gracious,' I thought, 'who in the world is that?" I was surprised, because nearly everybody came to the side door, which was habitually used by the tradespeople, and naturally we did not get other callers at this early hour. Indeed, we had very few callers at any time.

I listened at the top of the stairs and heard the maid Valentine go to the door. Then there was the sound of a man's voice, and I heard him say, "Is

Dr Crippen at home?" Valentine understood very little English, and, to my annoyance, I heard her say ' Yes "

"What a stupid creature that is!'" I said to myself, and then went part of the way downstairs, when I saw two men standing at the front door That was my first meeting with Inspector Dew, who was accompanied by Sergeant Mitchell Of course I had not the faintest idea who they were or what they wanted

" You wish to see Dr Crippen?' I asked

' Yes," replied Inspector Dew

"He is not at home," I said, "and will not return until after six o'clock this evening "

Inspector Dew looked at me in a curious way and said, "I beg your pardon, but I am informed that Dr Crippen is still here, and I wish to see him on important business "

" Well, you have been wrongly informed," I said "Dr Crippen always goes to his office shortly after eight o'clock "

" I am sorry to doubt your word," said Inspector Dew, "but I am given to understand that Dr Crippen does not go to his office until after eleven. I feel quite sure he is in the house, and I may as well tell you at once I shall not go until I have seen him Perhaps if I tell you who I am you will find Dr Crippen for me "

He then told me he was Inspector Dew and that his companion was Sergeant Mitchell I was naturally surprised to discover who they were, but I did not give them much thought at the time

"All the same," I said, "I cannot find Dr Crippen for you He is out

I was now quite angry It annoyed me to think that this man should flatly contradict me, and practically accuse me of telling an untruth

"You will have to stay a long time if you want to see him here,' I went on "He will not be home until after six this evening As you decline to believe me when I say he is not at home you had better come inside and look for him '

"Thank you," said Inspector Dew, "I will come inside '

The two men thereupon entered and went into the sitting-room They had not yet told me their business, and I was wondering what on earth they wanted.

Inspector Dew repeated several times that his business was most important, that he would not leave the place until he had spoken with the doctor, and that he would be much obliged if I would fetch him, "like a sensible little lady " I laughed at him, for after his first brusque manner this reference to my good sense was to be taken as a compliment

After my assurances, again, that the doctor was not at home, Inspector Dew declared that it was absolutely necessary in Dr Crippen's own interests that they should see him at once

I was startled at this What did detectives want with the doctor? What was this important affair about which there could be no delay? I suggested that I should telephone to him at his office, but this did not suit them   No, they would prefer me to go with them to the office

"All right," I said   "But you must give me time to dress properly "

"Certainly," said Inspector Dew   "We will wait for you "

I went upstairs into the bedroom, considering still whatever could have happened   I had no compunction in making them wait a good long time while I arranged my hair, put on a blouse, and generally made myself look presentable   Constantly I heard one or other of the men go to the door and listen at the sound of any footstep, yet, as I had explained to them, there was no possibility of anyone getting out of the house without their knowledge

Again and again the question came into my brain, "What do these people want? ' I racked my head about it, fairly puzzled   Yet I can honestly say that I was not much alarmed—only a little bewildered and more than a little annoyed

When I went downstairs again Inspector Dew was very affable and friendly, and inclined for conversation

' Come and sit down on the sofa " he said   " I would very much like to ask you a few questions "

His questions related to the time of my coming to Hilldrop Crescent, all my knowledge as to the date

MR. P. D. MUIR OPENING THE CASE FOR THE CROWN

upon which Mrs Crippen had gone away, and as to when I had heard the news of her death I answered quite simply and straightforwardly I had no desire to prevaricate, in spite of my annoyance with these mysterious visitors I could not remember exactly the date I had come to live at the Crescent, it was some time in February As for the news of Mrs Crippen's death, the doctor had told me of the cables stating that she had been taken ill, and then had died

"Did you see the cables ?" asked Inspector Dew

"No, I said "Why should I? I do not doubt Dr Crippen's word"

"Ah,' said Inspector Dew, in his curious way He was always saying that little word "ah ' as though he knew so much more than I did.

We had another little quarrel again about leaving the house and going to the office I told him frankly I was a person of methodical habits, and did not like having all my usual programme of the day upset in this fashion

"No, I quite understand that," said Inspector Dew, ' but you see this is a matter of very special importance to Dr Crippen It is for his sake, you see "

Of course there was nothing to do but fall in with their wishes, and together we left the house, took the electric tramcar to the Euston Road, and then a taxi-cab to Albion House. It was then a little after eleven

"Look here,' I said "I would not be a bit surprised if we did not find Dr Crippen there. He may be at the other office in Kingsway at this time"

Inspector Dew looked rather serious at this "We will take Albion House first," he said "I very much hope he will be there'

When we arrived I said, in the hall, "I do not propose to go upstairs with you two gentlemen I shall have to pass through two rooms where everybody knows me, and there will be a lot of talk and questions if I go all about the place with you You had better let me go and tell the doctor to come down to you"

This did not seem at all satisfactory to them, and they pressed me to let them come upstairs at once But I pointed out that there were only two doors of exit, and they could watch both at the same time. I did this with a smile, for the whole thing sounded to me so absurd I was beginning to regard the matter as a joke However, my words reassured Inspector Dew

"Yes, that will be all right," he said "You go up and tell the doctor"

I ascended in the lift, went through a couple of rooms, nodded a "Good morning" to my friends, and found Dr Crippen with Mr Rylance working at some gold plate for dental purposes I just touched him on the arm, and he looked up quite calmly, but just a little surprised at my appearance

"Hallo!" he said 'what's the matter?"

I whispered to him, "Come out, I want to speak to you

"What is it?" he asked, when he had followed me outside

Then I told him "There are two men from Scotland Yard They want to see you on important business For heaven's sake, come and talk to them They have been worrying me for about two hours"

"From Scotland Yard?" said Dr Crippen "That's very odd What do they want?"

Not a shade of expression passed over his face, except a faint surprise He showed no sign of fear or agitation He was absolutely calm He went down and brought the detectives up into his office Before the door was shut upon them Inspector Dew turned to me and said, "Don't go away I shall want to speak to you again when I have finished with Dr Crippen"

It was then about half-past eleven I went into another room, where I found Mr Long, the assistant, whom I have already mentioned We have had many jokes together

He jerked his thumb towards the inner room

"Who are they?" he said "What do they want?"

"I don't know," I said wearily

"Well," said Mr Long, "I don't mind saying those two men have come from a place called Scotland Yard"

"How on earth did you know?" I said laughing "You have guessed it at once"

"I know the stamp," said Mr Long "What's the trouble?"

"I can't imagine," I said "It's rather both-ing All I know is that I must not leave the office They want to see me again"

But I had not the least idea how long I should have to wait The half hours passed and the hour, and I became very hungry The detectives took the doctor out to lunch, forgetting me and I saw them come back again Meanwhile I was absolutely fainting with hunger

"I wish to goodness these people would come out," I said several times

At last they did It was then about a quarter to four, and Inspector Dew told me that it was now my turn

I was with him for an hour, and then for the first time I learnt that the trouble was about Mrs Crippen When I answered him questions about Belle Elmore, and told him again the doctor's story to me of her disappearance, her illness and her death, Inspector Dew turned to me suddenly, and said "He told you a lie He has just admitted to us that, as far as he knows, his wife was still alive, and that the story of her death in America was all an invention"

I was stunned I could not believe it It seemed impossible to me that Belle Elmore might still be alive Had I not the doctor's word? Surely he would not have deceived me! Oh, surely not! Stricken with grief, with anger, with bewilderment, I answered all the questions put to me about my relations with the doctor, my love for him, and my

life   But all the time I was thinking of the way I
had been deceived if this story about Mr. Crippen
were true

At six o'clock we all drove in a taxi-cab to
Hilldrop Crescent   I was silent   I seemed to be
living in a nightmare   I felt rather faint and sick
I understood that we were returning to the house,
and that the detectives were going to make a search
What was all this mystery?   The woman had gone
away   That I believed   Of that I was convinced
Yet I was very, very sorry that the doctor should
have told me an untruth about the matter

While the mysterious search was going on in the
house at Hilldrop Crescent I sat in the sitting-room,
listening, but quite stupefied and dazed   What were
these men doing?   Would they never go?   It grew
dark, and I sat there in the gloom   My head was
aching furiously   Since seven o'clock in the morning
I had had nothing to eat except a sandwich or two,
and it is no wonder that, with all this mystery and
anxiety, I felt quite ill

At last, about eight o'clock, the detectives left,
and Dr. Crippen and I were alone   That was a
relief, but I am bound to say that I was angry and
hurt, and that I felt in no mood for conversation
One thought only was in my head   It was, that the
doctor had told me a lie   He had been untruthful
to me for the first time in ten years—to me, of all
people in the world, who was certainly the one to
know the truth and all the truth   I had been
faithful to him   I loved him   I had given up all

MR. A. A. TOBIN, K.C., DEFENDING DR. CRIPPEN

things for him, and it hurt me frightfully that he should have deceived me

He tried to cheer me up   He begged me to take some supper, and we sat down together but I could eat nothing   I could even say nothing   I could not think   At about ten o clock I went up to my room, utterly weary in mind and body   I was too tired, too distracted, to undress then   I sat down in a chair, and presently the doctor came up   I then asked him a straight question

"For mercy's sake," I said, "tell me whether you know where Belle Elmore is   I have a right to know "

"I tell you truthfully," he said, "that I don't know where she is '

He repeated this several times   He had not the least idea he said, as to her whereabouts   She had gone off suddenly, as she had often threatened to do, and no word had come from her   He believed that she had disappeared for ever from his life

I was in no mood for discussing it further, and there we left the matter for the night

When I woke up next morning all that had happened on the previous day came back to my mind, but seemed utterly unreal   The doctor and I had a very serious conversation

He explained to me that the stories he had made up to account for the disappearance of Belle Elmore and his ignorance of her whereabouts would now be revealed to everybody, following upon the detectives' visit and that a tremendous scandal would be

caused   As he said the members of the Music Hall
Ladies' Guild, who had already been very inquisitive
about her, would all be talking and gossiping, and
that neither he nor I would be able to face the office
again   He thought only of me   He said that the
scandal would be far worse for me than for him, and
that he would do anything to save me from it

"Well, what is your idea?" I said   "What do
you think of doing?"

"My dear," he said, "there seems to me only
one thing possible to do, and that is to get away
We must leave all these prying people who will talk
about you and go somewhere until the whole affair
has blown over   The worst of it is, the police will
try to hold me here until she is found   Inspector
Dew said he must find Belle Elmore"

After some discussion he suggested that a disguise would be necessary

' But what sort of a disguise,' I asked

"Well, you would do very well as a boy," he
said   ' You have often told me how you played the
tomboy in your early years '

I did not like the idea at all   It seemed to me
that my tomboy days were over, and that it was not
well to begin again.   Could I dare to go about in
boy's clothes?   The doctor asked me to leave the
matter to him   He would arrange all about it   He
would also see after any luggage we might have to
take, but in any case it would be better to slip away
with as few things as possible

The whole affair seemed to me inexplicable, but

I fell in with his wishes   I had no idea of anything beyond this ..... o suspicion of any darke. secret   I told .'   that I had faith in him and trust in him   he went I would go That he thought was for the best would be the best for me   After all, he had been all in all to me, and I believed that he was doing everything for my sake rather than for his own

He told me the police had been questioning him closely about the jewellery worn by Belle Elmore They wanted to know whether he had disposed of it   This made me feel rather uneasy, for I recalled that it was owing to my advice that he had pawned it   But anyhow it was, I thought, a small matter

I had arranged for my young brother Sidney to spend the week-end with us   So I left a note for him with Valentine, telling him that I had been compelled to go away

We left the house after breakfast, carrying with us only one handbag containing a few articles, and went in the ordinary way to the office   I told the doctor that there was one thing I must do before going away, and that was to see my sister

"Certainly,' said Dr. Crippen   "I think you ought to do that "

' And I shall have to explain the thing to her, and tell her my reason for going off so suddenly "

"Yes," said Dr Crippen   "That is all right; but you must not stay talking too long '

From the office I took a taxi-cab to my sister's

DR. CRIPPEN TELLING HIS STORY IN THE WITNESS BOX.

house She opened the door to me, and was astonished to see me

"What is the matter?" she asked "Why do you look so pale?"

"I have come to say good-bye," I said "I am going away with the doctor!"

"Going away? Where? Why?"

"Oh, Nina," I said, "something awful has happened You know how Belle Elmore was supposed to have died? They say now that she is alive '

"Alive?" answered my sister. "Who says so?"

I told her about the visit of the detectives, and how the doctor had admitted to them that he had made up the stories regarding her death and did not know where she was

"There will be an awful scandal," I said, "and we are going away until it has blown over"

My sister was very much upset

"But you will come back afterwards?"

"Yes, of course I will come back," I said

At the end of our talk, which was all very hurried, she kissed me and wished me good luck I was feeling very distressed, and felt awful on the way back to the office

When I rejoined Dr Crippen he had got the boy's suit for which he had sent out Mr Long It was the brown suit which caused so much interest when it was held up in court In justice to Mr Long I think I ought to say that he had no reason whatever to be suspicious about this errand, because the doctor had not infrequently bought clothes for young fellows " down on their luck " He was always good to people in distress

When the new suit was produced by Dr Crippen he was very much amused

" You will look a perfect boy in that," he said " Especially when you have cut off your hair "

" Have I got to cut my hair ? " I cried

" Why, of course," he said, gaily " That is absolutely necessary '

Honestly, I was more amused than anything It seemed to me an adventure

In our private room I slipped off my girl's clothes, leaving them in a pile on the floor just as they had fallen and stepped into my boy's suit It was not a very good fit It was ludicrous I split them down the back at the very outset I laughed then at the absurdity, and, in spite of all my troubles, I smile now when I think of my first attempt at masquerading as a boy

The whole costume was complete—shirt, braces, waistcoat, trousers, jacket, collar and tie, boots and bowler hat Dr Crippen was just as gay as I was at this transformation It seemed a merry joke to him. Then he took up a large pair of office scissors

" Now for the hair," he said, and with one or two snips my " mop " fell to the floor It did not affect me as some people may imagine I did not think twice about this loss of my locks It was all part of the adventure. I put on the bowler hat, and walked up and down the room to get used to myself in such strange attire.

"I shall never be able to face the world in these things," I said.

I was like a child, and strutted up and down, and very soon felt quite at ease, although for a time I missed the habit of holding my skirt.

Dr. Crippen said, "You will do famously. No one will recognise you. You are a perfect boy!"

"I don't think I shall get on in the streets," I said. "I haven't the pluck to go out."

Yet I screwed up my courage, and after arranging a plan with the doctor I went down the winding staircase alone. To play the part more perfectly I had a lighted cigarette in my mouth—another novelty for me which I did not much appreciate.

Our scheme was for me to go ahead and meet the doctor outside the Tube station at Chancery Lane. Looking back on it now, it seems to me extraordinary that I should have gone down the steps of Albion House, where I had been for years, without being recognised, and that I should have passed through the streets without a soul suspecting that I was a girl in disguise. But, as a matter of fact, nobody paid the slightest attention to me.

I was terribly self-conscious, but the crowds surged past, and my disguise did not cause one man to turn his head. I suppose I must have had a certain amount of pluck. I was highly strung with

excitement, and the adventure was amusing to me
Yet I was nervous when I waited outside the Tube
station at the top of Chancery Lane The doctor
joined me there, and I noticed that he had shaved
off his moustache

"Do you recognise me?' he said, smiling, and
I told him that I would know him anywhere

We took the Tube to the Bank, and went to
Liverpool Street Station, where we found that the
train to Harwich, which the doctor proposed to take,
did not go until five o'clock We had just missed
one

It was then just after two, so that we had three
hours to pass somehow or somewhere

"Let us have a 'bus ride," said the doctor, and I
agreed willingly enough Strange as it may seem,
I was now quite cheerful, and, indeed, rather
exhilarated in spirits

It seemed to me that I had given the slip, in fine
style, to all those people who had been prying upon
my movements I had gone in disguise past their
very door in Albion House, and no longer would
they be able to scan me up and down with their
inquisitive eyes That made me feel glad, and I had
no thought whatever of any reason for escape except
this flight from scandal

I was getting quite at home with myself in boy's
clothes, and Dr Crippen said I looked a pretty boy
Where we went on that 'bus ride I have not a very
clear idea I think it was somewhere out at
Hackney I know that one way I rode on top of

the omnibus and the other way inside, and spoke only a few words lest my voice should betray me

After that we returned to Liverpool Street and caught the train to Harwich, and I then learnt from the doctor that we were going to cross over to the Hook of Holland   I did not mind where we were going   One place was as good as another to me, so long as I was with Dr Crippen   Always I had trust in him and relied upon his judgment and his kindness to me

There were very few passengers in the train, and only one in our carriage, who took no notice of me. I curled myself up in the corner and gave myself up to my own thoughts, only smiling now and again to my companion   Occasionally I thought of the wildness of the affair, the abandonment of my ordinary life, the mystery about the disappearance of Mrs Crippen, but, frankly, I was more interested in my disguise, and filled with the excitement of this adventure

We reached Harwich about half-past six, and had supper in the hotel adjoining the station, where we waited for the night boat, which started at nine o'clock

Dr Crippen was quite cheerful, and chaffed me a good deal about my appearance, and seemed to be free from worry   His kindness and his light-hearted conversation kept me from brooding over the mystery   Indeed, at that time there was no further sense of mystery to my mind   Belle Elmore had gone off somewhere or other, and would never enter our lives again And we were bound for foreign parts until the scandal had died down That was all, and all my love for Dr Crippen induced me to forgive his having hidden the exact truth from me

It was a pleasant crossing that night to the Hook Of course, it was not my first voyage I have already described how I went to Dieppe and Boulogne, and I had never felt sea-sick

I slept part of the night, and awakened feeling fresh and cheerful as we reached the Hook at five o'clock in the morning We had breakfast there, and left at seven o'clock on the train to Rotterdam

Here we spent practically the whole of the day, and the old Dutch town, which was quite new to me, interested me immensely We wandered about the quiet old canals, looked at the quaint houses, explored the side streets, watched the Dutchmen in their baggy trousers and big wooden shoes, and afterwards went to the Zoological Gardens, where we amused ourselves listening to the screeching of the parrots on their perches, and staring at the wild beasts In spite of being dressed as a boy, I was just a girl, full of high spirits, and greatly pleased at this exploration in a foreign city

During the day Dr Crippen suggested that I had better pay a visit to a barber's shop, as his attempt at hairdressing had been rough and ready, and my ragged locks were really rather straggling

"All right," I said, ' come along, but I don't quite like it "

Still, in I went to the nearest barber's shop along

our way, and, with a boldness which now seems to me impossible, sat down in a vacant chair The Dutch barber received me most politely, and after casting an expert eye upon my hair, which must have seemed to him somewhat long for a " lad " of my age, decided upon the clippers Good gracious ! how startled I was when I first felt the little instrument running up and down my head, and my hair scattering on the floor " Heavens, alive,' I thought, " I shall soon have no hair left at this rate ! '

Dr Crippen had taken a chair, and was watching the operation with secret amusement I could see his face in the mirror opposite to me When I came out with a poll as closely cropped as Jack Sheppard we both burst out laughing

Then for a time we sat outside a café, and here I was much amused by another little experience Two Dutch girls fell in love with me at first sight

" Oh, the pretty English boy ! ' they said in my own tongue, and much more in their own language which I could not understand But there was no mistaking the meaning of the eyes they cast at me ! It was Sunday morning, and I suppose these little Dutch girls, who were about sixteen years of age, were on their way to Sunday school.

Dr Crippen laughed very much, and said that in my disguise I looked a boy of about sixteen I was now wearing a straw hat, which I had brought with me in a paper bag, for in the hurry of getting off the boat I had left my bowler underneath the seat of one of the cabins

We left Rotterdam in the evening, and arrived that night at Brussels. That city was our home for ten days, and I can truly say that they were very happy days, on the whole, without a thought of peril or the horrors that were to follow. I was quite used to my boy's clothes now, and found them very comfortable, so that I had no worry about my disguise.

Again, I was delighted at the exploration of a foreign city. I explored it with my companion, north and south, east and west, and in the country parts beyond. Dr. Crippen showed no sign of nervousness or any desire to keep me indoors at the Hotel des Ardennes, where we put up. Never did he express a wish for me to avoid public places. Never did he evince a trace of anxiety about himself.

We saw all the sights that Brussels has to offer. Many times we went to the Exhibition, and wandered about the palaces and the side-shows, and had good fun in the old Flemish fair, and watched the crowds of foreign people about us. We went to the picture galleries, the museums, and the public gardens. On many fine days we spent charming hours among the trees and on the lawns of the Bois de la Cambre, listening to the band and the singing of the birds. It all seemed very beautiful, very peaceful, and they were happy days.

Yet, at last, I grew tired of Brussels. I had exhausted all the shop windows, which I had gazed into at first with such delight, and now I wanted

to move on somewhere else   I told this to
Dr Crippen, and he said, "Tired of Brussels
already ? Very well, we will push on   How about
Paris ?"

I said, "No, not Paris   Somewhere else "

Here I ought to explain that I had had no news
of what was happening in England   Dr Crippen
used to read "L'Etoile Belge" and other Belgian
papers, but they were all Greek to me, and I could
not understand them, although, as I have said, I
knew a little conversational French   I asked him
several times to try and get an English paper, but
he never did

I now know that there was a hue and cry after
us, that the English papers were full of reports
about us, and that descriptions of us were being
published broadcast   Yet never once did our names
in print come before my eyes   Never once did I
see a poster offering a reward for our discovery
I was utterly ignorant, utterly innocent, of everything

Our journey to Quebec was determined in a quite
accidental way   Dr Crippen had an idea of getting
back to Hull, crossing over to Liverpool, and getting
away to America from that port   But one day
when we were wandering about we saw an adver-
tisement of the *Montrose* steaming from Antwerp
to Quebec   Dr Crippen said, "That is what we
will do   Let us book berths on the *Montrose*, and
go over to Canada "

We inquired at the shipping office on July 17,

LORD ALVERSTONE, THE LORD CHIEF JUSTICE, WHO TRIED
THE CASE

and learnt that the *Montrose* would leave Antwerp
on the 20th We left Brussels, therefore, on the
19th spent the night at Antwerp, and caught the
boat in the morning

It was without the slightest sensation of nervousness that I stepped on board the big steamer in my
boy's clothes The change of scene seemed to me a
delightful thing to look forward to and just as I had
gone on board the boat at Harwich with only a
sense of adventure, so now I was quite easy and free
from care when I followed Dr Crippen on to the
deck of the *Montrose* He also to all outward
appearance, was calm and untroubled He did not
for one moment lead me to believe that he was
afraid of being arrested Yet at that very time, I
am told, all the great ports were being watched by
detectives

If I had known of the frantic search that was
being made for us, I should have understood that we
were very badly prepared for a secret voyage Our
lack of luggage was in itself calculated to betray us
We only had with us the one handbag which we had
brought from Hilldrop Crescent As for myself, I
had nothing beyond my boy's suit— not even an
overcoat The doctor was wearing his grey frock
coat and his soft white hat I think it was at this
time that he left off his glasses

Beyond ourselves there were few English passengers They were mainly foreign emigrants, and,
like ourselves, hoping to begin life again in the New
World We had taken a second-class cabin, which

was quite cosy, and to me the whole ship was wonderful I found plenty to amuse me, for Captain Kendall supplied me with plenty of literature in the shape of novels and magazines, not forgetting some detective stories

I spent many hours on deck with Dr Crippen, but, naturally, I kept rather aloof from the other passengers, and did not speak very much On the other hand, when any of the officers spoke to me I did not hesitate to reply, and did not feel in the least embarrassed It never entered my head that they had discovered my disguise I felt so sure of myself I remember there was one nice English boy with whom I got rather chummy We used to talk football together ' Afterwards Dr Crippen laughingly said ' How nicely you are getting on ! "

At this time, as all the world knows, Scotland Yard was signalling to the *Montrose* by wireless I might have heard the ticking of the instrument, and, of course, I noticed the wires up aloft, but I did not pay any attention to them, nor did I guess that Inspector Dew was whispering to the captain and receiving answers It seems wonderful as I think of it

But we suspected nothing The doctor was as calm as ever, and spent as much time in reading as myself He was very friendly with Captain Kendall and at meal times many amusing stories were told over the table, which kept us in a good humour All the officers were very courteous to us, and used often to ask me how I was getting on

When I left my sister on that Saturday morning I promised her that I would write as soon as we were settled I thought that she would be wondering what had become of me As I touched land I promised myself that I would write her a long letter—oh ! such a letter ! I had been saving up all my little adventures in Rotterdam and Brussels How she would laugh at my boyish escapade How she would marvel at my impudence ! Alas ! that letter was never written.

I was kept in my cabin a good deal The weather was becoming very cold, and, as I had no overcoat, I began to feel that my boy's suit was altogether too thin for the climate on deck So with a rug wrapped round me I used to tuck into a corner of the lounge with a novel before me, and read quite fanciful adventures, which now I know were not so romantic as my own I was as happy as I could expect to be

Now, almost at the very end of our trip, I noticed a change in Dr Crippen Two days before we reached Father Point, just off Quebec, he came down to the cabin very serious Before we left London I had handed him all my money, now changed into notes and amounting to £15

" My dear,' he said, " I think you had better take charge of these "

" Why ?' I exclaimed, " I have nowhere to put them except in these pockets You can keep them, can't you, until you get to Quebec ? "

"Well," he said, hesitatingly, "I may have to leave you '

"Leave me!" I said I was astounded It seemed to me incredible that I should have come all this way and then should be left alone

"Listen, dear,' he said "When you get to Quebec you had better go on to Toronto It is a nice place and I know it fairly well You have not forgotten your typewriting, have you, and you have got your millinery at your fingers' ends?"

It then occurred to me that what he meant was that he should go ahead and prospect the country in order that we might settle down in peace in some out-of-the-way spot

"But," I said, now easier in my mind, "how about these clothes?"

"Are you tired of being a boy?' he asked, smiling at me

"Well, I am rather,' I replied "I used to imagine I would make a good boy, but now I do not think I fit the part I want to get into girl's clothes as quickly as I can"

"Very well you can buy them when you land"

"But I cannot do that It would be absurd for me to go into a shop dressed as a boy to buy women's garments You will have to get them

"Ah, I hadn't thought about that," he said, getting serious again He turned the matter over in his mind for some moments, and then said "Immediately on landing we must go to an hotel I will go out and get some clothes for you, and you will have to do a quick change   Then you will leave and I will follow you out "

I agreed to this, and went on reading my book.

A story has been told that we formed a plot to commit suicide, and so end our worries.   As a matter of fact, this was not so, for the very reason that I had no great trouble, and I looked forward with keen delight to an adventurous life in Canada I had not the faintest suspicion of the police pursuit

I remember on that fateful Sunday morning that Dr Crippen pressed me after breakfast to go on deck with him

" I don't think I will," I said   " It's very wretched up there, and I would rather stay down here and finish this book before lunch "

He went away quietly   Little did I know that I should not speak to him again for many days

A little time passed, and then the blow fell There was a tap at the cabin door   I turned round quite naturally, expecting to see the doctor again. Instead I saw Inspector Dew !   Even in his pilot's garb I did not fail to recognise him instantly.

The sight of him stunned me   At this moment, for the first time, I realised that there was something dreadful amiss   That this inspector should have chased us all the way from England filled me with horrible forebodings   I gave a cry, and then fell into a swoon

When I recovered I heard Inspector Dew read

MR. F. E SMITH, K C , M P , SPEAKING IN DEFENCE OF
MISS LE NEVE.

out his warrant for my arrest   I heard something
about the "murder and mutilation' of Mrs Crippen
as in a dream   What it meant I did not know
Lately I had been thinking that Belle Elmore was
alive, after all, and I had resolved when we reached
Canada to confront the person who had sent the
cablegrams to Dr Crippen   Now I was given to
understand that not only was she dead, but murdered!
Not only murdered, but that I was charged with
being a party to the crime—a crime about which I
knew absolutely nothing

Can it be wondered at that I was paralysed with
fear and astonishment?   I could say nothing   I
could think of nothing   I dared not ask even about
Dr Crippen, and we were kept rigidly apart   What
followed is a long and dreadful nightmare

Our landing at Quebec was anything but the
cheerful arrival which I had anticipated   We were
hurried ashore through a crowd of curious sightseers
to the prison on Abraham's Plain   There, of course,
I saw nothing of my dear doctor   People were kind
to me, but I was stupefied   I was kept some part
of the time in the house of Mr McCarthy, the
Canadian detective who had assisted Inspector Dew
on the *Montrose*

Inspector Dew himself visited me from time to
time, and was terribly nervous lest I should endeavour
to do desperate things   Very soon after my arrival
at Quebec I cast off my boy's suit, and I was extremely glad to get again into girl's clothes, kindly
bought for me by Inspector Dew.

It was whilst I was at Quebec that I learned for the first time of the discovery of human remains in the coal cellar at Hilldrop Crescent A day or two after our arrival Inspector Dew handed me a cable from my father advising me to tell everything

"You see what your father says," remarked Inspector Dew

'I assure you, Mr Dew," I said, "I know nothing about this Neither by word nor deed on the part of Dr Crippen have I been allowed to guess that anything was seriously wrong"

'Well,' said Inspector Dew, "I found human remains underneath the floor of the coal cellar at Hilldrop Crescent"

I was mystified, and could simply stare at him in amazement We never discussed the matter again

I heard Dr Crippen was brought up at the court in Quebec, but I myself was never taken there Afterwards the judge came to see me at Mr McCarthy's house, and was very polite to me He asked me if I wished to go back to England without delay, and I said, "Yes, certainly"

Altogether we were nineteen days in Quebec, and I found the waiting very dreary I began quite to look forward to returning to London

About a week before we left Inspector Dew came and said, "I want you to be up and ready at six o'clock every morning now in case I come for you."

At last the day of our departure came round I was removed from the prison at six o clock in the morning and t ken on a seven miles' drive in a closed carriage—with the blinds down—to Levis   There I v as put on board a launch, and also Dr Crippen, but I did not see him then

We had a long trip down the St Lawrence River to meet the *Megantic*, with a boat containing journalists giving a hot pursuit   It was very exciting, and Inspector Dew got a bit anxious

At last we came alongside the *Megantic*, which was waiting for us, and in Inspector Dew s great-coat to baffle the photographers, I was put on board and hurried to a cabin.

In a few minutes—Dr Crippen having followed —we started for England   Oh, that way back! The contrast to the outward voyage was like that between night and morning   The two wardresses who had been sent out to guard me never relaxed their vigilance   At night one of them always sat up with me while the other slept

Even now I think of one or two amusing incidents which relieved the monotony   Inspector Dew, who was always very kind, used to visit us often, and he was so paternal in his manner that we got accustomed to calling him " Father "

" Dear me, ' father ' is very grand to-night, ' we used to say when the inspector put on his evening dress and dined with the general company in the state saloon

When nearing Ireland we encountered very rough weather, and we all felt the effects of it Inspector Dew himself fell a victim to sea-sickness

On the landing-stage at Liverpool there was so great a crowd that I was really lost! The Canadian soldiers who had travelled over with us kept the throng back when it threatened to separate me and the two wardresses from the detectives who were in front in charge of Dr Crippen

It was only as I entered the train that I caught a glimpse of the doctor, huddled up between his guards His look was very wistful, and saddened me I nodded to him and smiled just to cheer him up, and his face brightened very much At Euston there was another very large crowd to witness our arrival But here, I am glad to say, I was allowed to walk across the platform just like an ordinary passenger to the taxi-cab which was waiting to convey me to the street

When we reached the police-station we were taken at once into the charge-room There Dr Crippen and I stood side by side while the same dreadful words about ' murder and mutilation " were read out

The next time I saw the doctor was when we passed into the dock at the police-court to begin the terrible ordeal of a public trial Even in those painful surroundings it was a comfort to me to be near him again Now and then we whispered together, but, unfortunately, Dr Crippen is a little deaf in the left ear, and that was nearest to me, so that we could only have a few snatches of conversation

At the police-court during the week which

followed I heard the full details of the discovery at Hilldrop Crescent   All the time the evidence seemed to me utterly unreal and past belief   I could not associate the doctor with cruelty or crime I knew him only as a man of tenderness and gentle nature, and it is thus that I now think of him

It was thus that I thought of him when I sat in my lonely cell at the Old Bailey waiting wearily day after day while his trial was going on in the court above   They allowed me to read the papers, and into my brain there burnt those dreadful things brought against him by the Crown

When his ordeal was over they drove me away in complete ignorance of his fate   I was yearning to know the verdict, but it was kept from me   It was two days afterwards when the Governor of Holloway Prison broke the news to me

Oh ! my poor broken heart !

I have been thinking of him always more than of myself   The thought that he had been sentenced to death outweighed in my mind altogether the knowledge that my own trial was yet to come   I am thankful it was short   I had left Holloway Prison in the morning with all sorts of good wishes, and I, myself, had no fear as to the result   I knew in my heart that I was perfectly innocent

But while Mr Muir was speaking for the prosecution I thought he was making things look very black for me   The mere fact of my going off disguised as a boy seemed to him to suggest a guilty mind   I was reassured however by the speech of my counsel, Mr F E Smith—which, I thought, was simply splendid—and still more by the summing-up of the judge

As the jury filed out to consider their verdict, my solicitor told me not to worry any more It would be all right! And, sure enough, it was With the verdict of " Not guilty " ringing in my ears I passed down the stairs at the back of the dock—down which the doctor had passed three days previously a convicted man—to liberty

In a room below I was quickly joined by my sister and her husband, who have never wavered in their devotion to me   Then, while a large crowd was waiting in the street in the expectation of seeing me, I was taken along devious passages to a side door, where we were able to get away in a taxi-cab absolutely unnoticed

Oh ! how relieved I was to be out in the streets of London once more   My joy at finding myself free again was, however, tempered with the knowledge that away in Pentonville Prison the friend who had brought so much brightness into my life was lying under the shadow of death

Since then I have been permitted to see him, and his great composure, his obvious pleasure at seeing me again, and his tender solicitude for my future career, comforted me very much   I verily believe that even now he is concerned far less for himself than for me

     *   *   *   *   *

Here, then, is my story, told in all simplicity and in all truthfulness   All I hope is that, having read these words, the world will think of me with sympathy, and that I may be allowed the chance of redeeming my faults without the additional burden of unjust reproach

9 781275 309142